THE SCIENCE
OF
PERSONAL
ACHIEVEMENT

DR. AYODELE COLE BENSON
MB BCH, MSC, DHA, PHD

Halo
PUBLISHING
INTERNATIONAL

New Living Translation, second edition, Tyndale House
Publishers, Inc, Carol Stream, Illinois Copyright 2008

Scripture is taken from The Holy Bible King James Version

ISBN: 978-1-61244-804-6
Library of Congress Control Number: 2019919465

Printed in the United States of America

Halo Publishing International
8000 W Interstate 10
Suite 600
San Antonio, Texas 78230
www.halopublishing.com
contact@halopublishing.com

CONTENTS

APPRECIATION

My sincere gratitude to the Almighty God for His inspiration to put this material together, and to the inspirational teachings of Napoleon Hills. They demonstrate his ardent belief in the Holy Scriptures and provoked me to probe more deeply into these time-tested principles. I remain grateful to Dennis Roquand for putting those materials in my hands.

I say a big "thank you" to my ministers, the Rev. Joe Olaiya and Bishop David Abioye, who, despite their tight schedules, read through this manuscript, gave their insights, and wrote the forewords.

I appreciate my family, my wife Grace and my children Mordecai and Jemima, for their prayers, unrelenting help, and unflinching support in all my adventures. In particular, my son Mordecai Dominion Benson put together this manuscript and spent a good part of his holiday reviewing the final text. I am grateful.

Many thanks also to Lawrence Ezisi, an author, researcher, and ardent believer in youth empowerment whose research forms part of the text cited in this book.

I am blessed to have all of you who have added colour to this endeavour. Thank you so much.

FOREWORD I

A BOOK FOR TOP GUNNERS

This book is a masterpiece and resource for those who are gunning for the top. It will help you to reach your goals, get done what you want to get done, and bring forth the best of your dreams.

It is a step-by-step guide to transforming yourself into an achiever and to reaching your destiny gloriously. It is a blessing to all and sundry, believers included, who have great dreams, or dreams that appear impossible at heights that seem unattainable. This book will strengthen your drive and also equip you with the tools you need to accomplish great feats.

I recommend this book to those who are already succeeding, so that they can keep their success and do better. I especially recommend it to those who just want to take off to great heights. I most recommend it to those who have had some failures, stagnancy, or fruitless struggles. This book will be a great asset to transform your psyche, equip your mind, and strengthen your faith to achieve.

Please read repeatedly to get the best out of it. Beyond reading, ingrain these principles in your life pursuits. See you soon at the top!

Wishing you happy and fruitful reading,

The Rev. P. J. A. Olaiya

Kaduna, Nigeria

FOREWORD II

Achievement in life is the desire and dream of most individuals. Certainly, failure is not what anyone wants to identify with; it is abhorred and detested. Personal achievement, on the other hand, is a delight: It gives one confidence and a voice. That is why we all should aspire towards personal achievement in whatever we are doing!

However, while many look at achievement through the prism of circumstances that surround them—economic and geographical circumstances, etc.—and hence are ill-motivated to venture towards excellence, because of what they consider to be disadvantages, others, given the same situations and challenges, are breaking new ground and scaling higher heights. The difference is in their level of understanding of, attitude towards, and perspective on life. Besides, personal achievement is unobtainable without the setting of clear targets backed up by a strong drive towards attainment.

Among vital and resourceful tools for personal achievement are the books we read. Books widen our horizon and propel us towards a greater tomorrow, beyond whatever challenges that tend to keep us in the same spot. When diligently studied, books never leave people the same way they met them.

History books are replete with people who, via their pursuits and achievements, have contributed in no small measure to shaping our human existence. Through their laudable feats, life has become more interesting and enterprising. Also, strides are being taken for more result-oriented approaches to issues, rather than just allowing things to happen.

But, of all the books ever written about human existence, the Holy Bible is the only one widely referred to as the Book of Life. This is because its content addresses virtually all aspects of human evolution and developments. It is not just a spiritual book. Its precepts, laws, and principles are precise and applicable to all spheres of human endeavours and it has never needed to be reviewed. Obviously, the integration of biblical principles into our lives is vital to sustained personal achievement.

The author of this book, *The Science of Personal Achievement*, has done great work with his research into how great people succeed and become points of reference in life. At the same time, he buttresses his findings with historical facts from the pages of the Bible.

Through its pages, Dr. Ayodele Benson has put in your hand materials that will spur aspiration in you. It will spur you towards becoming the best you've ever desired in your career. It will offer hope to the despondent and give clarity of direction to the uncertainties of the future.

It is my prayer that you will draw inspiration from this book and find points of application to your life's situations as you go through each chapter of the book. May your life never remain the same again.

In Jesus' name,

Bishop David O. Abioye

Abuja, Nigeria

INTRODUCTION

This book is based on the findings of elaborate research conducted by Napoleon Hills in the early 1920s, which spanned a twenty-year period and profiled more than 500 successful people. Among them were captains of industry, past presidents, and major economic players in the United States and other parts of the world. His research focused on seeking an understanding of what made these individuals attain outstanding success.

Particularly, a lot of insight was drawn from the life of Andrew Carnegie, the richest man in the world at the time. Other notable people who were research subjects included Henry Ford, Thomas Edison, the Wright brothers, and some past presidents of the United States who were still living at the time.

Napoleon Hills documented the outcomes of his twenty years of research and summarised his findings in seventeen principles of personal success, which have been compressed in this book into thirteen notable laws of personal achievement. Despite the secular nature of the original research, further studies have established that all the principles discussed by Napoleon Hills have their roots in the pages of the Holy Bible.

This book, therefore, presents you with well-rounded rules of personal success which have been time-tested and proven to deliver success to those who utilize these tenets to achieve outstanding results. The biblical contexts have been given to establish the scriptural roots of all the principles, validating the fact that the Bible is truly the Book of Life. Contemporary examples are provided to show that, even in this information age, biblical principles remain valid and potent.

The science behind personal success is therefore established on the fact that obedience to key principles will deliver guaranteed-successful outcomes, irrespective of creed, race, profession, or social inclination. Another statement of fact is that success is relative. It is a journey with its destination determined only by the person embarking on the trip. You may, therefore, have attained remarkable success by your own assessment, but you can go somewhat further to positively impact more lives. On the other hand, you may just have commenced your journey towards success.

I am confident that, in each scenario, adherence to the lessons in this book will ensure that you are the next big success story.

PRINCIPLE 1:

A POSITIVE MENTAL ATTITUDE
AND DEFINITENESS OF PURPOSE

"An attitude of positive expectation is the mark of the superior personality."

Brian Tracy

Nature wants man to use his mind constructively, but this cannot be achieved without a positive mental attitude set off by a definite, major purpose. The prayers with effective results are those that are offered passionately and resolutely. The subconscious mind only finds opportunities to innovate when there is an optimistic mindset. How else does an accomplished lawyer convince the jury, if not with a positive mental attitude?

While a positive mental attitude looks for ways by which something can be achieved, a negative mental attitude makes excuses for the reasons something cannot be done. You have probably heard it said that the average person uses only 10% of his or her potential. The sad truth is that, according to Stanford University, the average person functions with only about 2% of his or her mental potential. The rest of that potential remains dormant and may never be utilized in a lifetime. Why have we accomplished too little as a people? The answer is simple: Where purpose is not defined with corresponding zeal, life gets uninspiring and failure becomes imminent.

You've got what it takes

You can develop and nurture a positive mental attitude by heeding these seven tried-and-true, easy instructions:

- You need to keep your mind charged to retain a positive mental attitude. Keep feeding the mind with the things you want and not the things you do not want. Boxing legend Muhammad Ali said this about himself: "I am the greatest." He later revealed, "I said that even before I knew I was."

- Associate with people with positive attitudes who would influence you towards a positive path. American author and entrepreneur Mark Twain warned: "Keep away from people who try to belittle your ambitions. Small people always do that, but the really great ones make you feel that you, too, can become great."

- Decide to do the things you want to do no, matter how hard the obstacles may be, because how you do anything is how you do everything.

A positive mental attitude is what controls who is attracted to you. Your mental attitude, not necessarily your speech, determines the type of people attracted to you. Even without speaking, your subconscious thoughts attract people to you, depending on what your dominant mental attitude is.

Your mental attitude determines whether you find peace of mind or you go through life with frustration. If you control your own mental attitude, you control every other thing in your life.

Unless you condition your mind to be a salesman with a positive mental attitude, you cannot make a sale. Unless you change how you are, you'll always get what you've got.

Definiteness of purpose, on the other hand, is the unwavering commitment towards the attainment of a clearly defined objective or a major goal.

It is comprised of turning on your willpower, with no desire to quit. In the face of opposition or challenges, instead of quitting, turn on more efforts. The easiest thing for a weakling to do is to quit.

George Weah of Liberia first sought the Liberian presidency in 2005 at age 39. He failed, then obtained his SSCE in 2006 at age 40, a university degree in 2011 at aged 45, and a Master's degree in 2013 at age 47. He won election to the Senate of Liberia in 2014 at age 48. He was eventually elected as the country's president, in 2017 at age 51, as a reward for his definiteness of purpose.

All this happened within 12 years. It clearly demonstrates that, when you make up your mind to succeed, you must also be willing to act on your convictions. It's never too late to start. Success lies is in taking one step at a time, with the goal in focus.

Perhaps no other person has paid the price for definiteness of purpose like the late Nelson Mandela. In his struggle for the freedom of South Africa from white domination and the apartheid regime, he spent 27 years of his life in an isolated prison cell on Robbins Island. During his court case, on April 20, 1964, before he was eventually jailed, read what he said as his closing statement after a very long defence submission during the Rivonia Trial:

"During my lifetime I have dedicated myself to this struggle of the African people. I have fought against white domination, and I have fought against black domination. I have cherished the ideal of

a democratic and free society in which all persons live together in harmony and with equal opportunities. It is an ideal which I hope to live for and to achieve. But if needs be, it is an ideal for which I am prepared to die."

Common knowledge reminds us that Nelson Mandela not only achieved his definite major purpose, he indeed lived to become the first black president of a free South Africa. Today, the nation of South Africa is enjoying the democracy and liberty of all people, which Nelson Mandela made his definite major purpose, despite all the tough odds that he had to face.

Human thoughts have the ability to transform themselves into physical existence. Inside of you are two people: a positive person and a negative person. It is the positive person in you that has the positive mental attitude that believes in personal achievement, success, love, and greatness. A positive mental attitude is the first of all riches.

It provides the platform for true friendship and friendly cooperation, it breeds the riches of personal achievement, it controls the riches of faith and self-belief.

Successful people are people who settle for nothing less than what they desire to accomplish. You must become success-conscious.

Factors required for the path to success:

- Define the purpose

- Develop a definite plan

- Adopt an action plan (how it will be achieved)

There are fears you must deal with in order to operate with definiteness of purpose. Sometimes people around you—family, friends, etc.—are the ones that instill the fear into you. But with definiteness of purpose, you must dismiss fear. Recognize that fears exist but do not dwell on them because, once you have a burning desire, you sleep with it and wake up with it. Soon it becomes registered in your subconscious mind. Any dominating desire is taken up by the subconscious part of the brain and is acted upon as if it already exists.

Joel 3:10b says: "Let the weak say, I am strong." And as you continue to say it in faith, it registers in your subconscious, and the mind-body connection will begin to infuse strength into your body cells.

The subconscious part of the brain acts as both a receiver and a transmitter. Hence, when you have a dominant plan of success in your subconscious, you begin to attract transmission from people operating on the same frequency. Hence, successful people get attracted to you because you are connected on a subconscious frequency.

The bible says, "Keep your heart with all diligence for out of it are the issues of your life" (Proverbs 4:23).

By making the mind positive, you free yourself from fears and anxiety. Back your desire with mental and physical action. Keep your mind off the things you do not desire because the mind attracts things that it feeds upon. Keep your mind free of greed, anger, jealousy, fear, sickness, and revenge.

How to develop definiteness of purpose:

- Write out your definite major purpose and read it to yourself several times a day.

- Develop an action plan.

- Keep your definite major purpose in your mind and recall it as often as you can. Once it gets into your subconscious mind, nature will act upon it, even when you are asleep.

- Focus on specifics and do not be vague. Give yourself a timeline on which to achieve your major purpose.

- Decide what you will give, or pay in return, for the achievement of your definite major purpose.

Nature frowns at the very idea of getting something for nothing.

Scriptural examples of the definiteness of purpose:

From the Old Testament to the New Testament, examples abound of people who had definite major purposes that they pursued until those goals were attained. Notable among so many are Elisha, David, Jesus, and the apostle Paul.

"And it came to pass, when the LORD would take up Elijah into heaven by a whirlwind, that Elijah went with Elisha from Gilgal.

And Elijah said unto Elisha, Tarry here, I pray thee; for the LORD hath sent me to Bethel. And Elisha said unto him, As the LORD liveth, and as thy soul liveth, I will not leave thee. So they went down to Bethel.

And the sons of the prophets that were at Bethel came forth to Elisha, and said unto him, Knowest thou that the LORD will take away thy master from thy head to day? And he said, Yea, I know it; hold ye your peace.

And Elijah said unto him, Elisha, tarry here, I pray thee; for the LORD hath sent me to Jericho. And he said, As the LORD liveth, and as thy soul liveth, I will not leave thee. So they came to Jericho.

And the sons of the prophets that were at Jericho came to Elisha, and said unto him, Knowest thou that the LORD will take away thy master from thy head to day? And he answered, Yea, I know it; hold ye your peace.

And Elijah said unto him, Tarry, I pray thee, here; for the LORD hath sent me to Jordan. And he said, As the LORD liveth, and as thy soul liveth, I will not leave thee. And they two went on.

And fifty men of the sons of the prophets went, and stood to view afar off: and they two stood by Jordan.

And Elijah took his mantle, and wrapped it together, and smote the waters, and they were divided hither and thither, so that they two went over on dry ground.

And it came to pass, when they were gone over, that Elijah said unto Elisha, Ask what I shall do for thee, before I be taken away from thee. And Elisha said, I pray thee, let a double portion of thy spirit be upon me.

And he said, Thou hast asked a hard thing: nevertheless, if thou see me when I am taken from thee, it shall be so unto thee; but if not, it shall not be so.

And it came to pass, as they still went on, and talked, that, behold, there appeared a chariot of fire, and horses of fire, and parted them both asunder; and Elijah went up by a whirlwind into heaven.

And Elisha saw it, and he cried, My father, my father, the chariot of Israel, and the horsemen thereof. And he saw him no more: and he took hold of his own clothes, and rent them in two pieces.

He took up also the mantle of Elijah that fell from him, and went back, and stood by the bank of Jordan;

And he took the mantle of Elijah that fell from him, and smote the waters, and said, Where is the LORD God of Elijah? and when he also had smitten the waters, they parted hither and thither: and Elisha went over.

And when the sons of the prophets which were to view at Jericho saw him, they said, The spirit of Elijah doth rest on Elisha. And they came to meet him, and bowed themselves to the ground before him." (2 Kings 2:1-15)

In this lengthy scriptural text, Elisha was resolute and definite in his quest to receive the double portion of the anointing of Elijah, to the point that nothing could discourage him.

Similarly, in 1 Samuel 17:19-52, the story is told of the battle of the Israelites against the Philistines. David was determined to fight the war champion of the Philistines, named Goliath, despite intimidation from David's own brothers, from Goliath himself, and even despite discouragement from Saul, the king. But see how David responded: "And David said to Saul, Let no man's heart fail because of him; thy servant will go and fight with this Philistine" (1 Samuel 17:32). The rest is history. We know the outcome of that event: David killed Goliath and freed Israel from the perpetual harassment and intimidation of the Philistines.

Concerning Jesus, He had a definite major purpose and always expressed it to His disciples:

"And he began to teach them, that the Son of man must suffer many things, and be rejected of the elders, and of the chief priests, and scribes, and be killed, and after three days rise again.

And he spake that saying openly. And Peter took him, and began to rebuke him.

But when he had turned about and looked on his disciples, he rebuked Peter, saying, Get thee behind me, Satan: for thou savourest not the things that be of God, but the things that be of men."
(Mark 8:31-33)

Individuals with definite major purposes do not take in the voices of discouragement. Rather, they rebuke discouragement sternly with no apologies. Indeed, they have a good habit of discouraging discouragement. They react appropriately, with a positive mental attitude, to anything that will cause fear. With the readiness to pay any price to attain the ultimate goal, definiteness of purpose overcomes fear.

Paul exemplified this when he reacted to the prophesies of imprisonment if he were to go to Jerusalem to preach the gospel: "But none of these things move me, neither count I my life dear unto myself, so that I might finish my course with joy, and the ministry, which I have received of the Lord Jesus, to testify the gospel of the grace of God" (Acts 20:24).

Much more can be said of these men and their demonstrations of definiteness of purpose but, for simplicity, these few instances have been chosen to showcase their characters. We have a lot to learn from them.

PRINCIPLE 2:

THE MASTERMIND ALLIANCE

"Coming together is the beginning. Keeping together is progress. Working together is success."

Henry Ford, Founder of the Ford Motor Company

A mastermind alliance is created when two or more people are working together, in harmony, with definiteness of purpose towards the attainment of a definite major objective.

When you connect your mind with other minds, you tap into their education, their resources, their influence, their networks, and their spiritual abilities. You cannot achieve much in life if you do not learn to use other people's money and other people's brains. Therefore, you should not do for yourself what someone else is able to do better for you. The scriptural root of this wisdom is seen in the act of Pharaoh putting Joseph in charge of the Kingdom of Egypt after the interpretation of his dreams.

"And Pharaoh said unto his servants, Can we find such a one as this is, a man in whom the Spirit of God is?

And Pharaoh said unto Joseph, Forasmuch as God hath shewed thee all this, there is none so discreet and wise as thou art:

Thou shalt be over my house, and according unto thy word shall all my people be ruled: only in the throne will I be greater than thou.

And Pharaoh said unto Joseph, See, I have set thee over all the land of Egypt.

And Pharaoh took off his ring from his hand, and put it upon Joseph's hand, and arrayed him in vestures of fine linen, and put a gold chain about his neck;

And he made him to ride in the second chariot which he had; and they cried before him, Bow the knee: and he made him ruler over all the land of Egypt.

And Pharaoh said unto Joseph, I am Pharaoh, and without thee shall no man lift up his hand or foot in all the land of Egypt."
(Genesis 41:38-44)

The mastermind alliance stimulates your mind to elevate your enthusiasm. That is why, when properly utilized, your mastermind alliance stimulates your mental attitude, it provides opportunities to increase your initiative and eliminate the emotion of fear.

Your mastermind alliance stimulates the spiritual powers of those within the alliance. That is why, in Acts of the Apostle, when they were threatened, they went back to their own company.

"And being let go, they went to their own company, and reported all that the chief priests and elders had said unto them.

And when they heard that, they lifted up their voice to God with one accord, and said, Lord, thou art God, which hast made heaven, and earth, and the sea, and all that in them is:

Who by the mouth of thy servant David hast said, Why did the heathen rage, and the people imagine vain things?

The kings of the earth stood up, and the rulers were gathered together against the Lord, and against his Christ.

For of a truth against thy holy child Jesus, whom thou hast anointed, both Herod, and Pontius Pilate, with the Gentiles, and the people of Israel, were gathered together,

For to do whatsoever thy hand and thy counsel determined before to be done.

And now, Lord, behold their threatenings: and grant unto thy servants, that with all boldness they may speak thy word,

By stretching forth thine hand to heal; and that signs and wonders may be done by the name of thy holy child Jesus.

And when they had prayed, the place was shaken where they were assembled together; and they were all filled with the Holy Ghost, and they spake the word of God with boldness."
(Acts 4:23-31)

When Daniel had the problem of interpreting the king's dream he went back to his three other friends to discuss the matter and to pray about it tapping into the spiritual abilities of each member of the alliance.

"Then Daniel went to his house, and made the thing known to Hananiah, Mishael, and Azariah, his companions:

That they would desire mercies of the God of heaven concerning this secret; that Daniel and his fellows should not perish with the rest of the wise men of Babylon.

Then was the secret revealed unto Daniel in a night vision. Then Daniel blessed the God of heaven." (Daniel 2:17-19)

A mastermind alliance can be used to great advantage in the home, between the husband and the wife, and also in the boardroom. One of the best-kept secrets of successful captains of industry is their regular application of the principle of the mastermind alliance. They consciously surround themselves with people who, in particular vocations, are smarter than they are. They basically encircle themselves with specialists from various fields and by so doing they benefit from a wealth of diverse knowledge and they become well-versed on how the business world works.

Small business owners should take a cue from them on how larger-scale businesses work. For small businesses, Fola Adeola, founder of Guaranty Trust Bank (GTBank), advised that a formal board of directors should not be considered for a business with less than 25 staff members, but that these smaller businesses could leverage informal boards.

Thus, his counsel was that a business owner should consider having one of the two types of boards, or both: the official board members and the unofficial board members—mentors or coaches that you look up to.

Fola told his mentees at a FATE Foundation summit about his early days as managing director of the bank. He used to drive down to Iganmu (in Lagos) to see two men, one of whom was a man called Felix Ohiwerei, who was then managing director of Nigerian Breweries, while the other, Christopher Kolade, was then with the Lagos Business School of Pan-Atlantic University. Both men, he said, served as members of his unofficial board. They offered him insights and free advice that enabled him to successfully pilot the affairs of the then-fledgling bank. They never sat on the bank's official board of directors with him.

Indeed, the Bible says, "Two are better than one for they get a better reward for all their labor" (Ecclesiastes 4:9).

Types of mastermind alliances:

• Social alliance. Example: family alliance, church, etc. No material gain is involved.

- Professional alliance. This is an alliance that has a definite motive between professional colleagues or individuals that have a common interest to benefit from.

Notes:

- Do not accept favors without the intention of returning such favors. Develop the habit of not getting something for nothing.

- Ensure that all members of the alliance have a definite benefit from the alliance.

- Maintain regular contact with members of your mastermind group.

- Ensure that harmony is maintained within the alliance governed by the definiteness of purpose.

The Bible says, "Two cannot walk together except they be agreed" (Amos 3:3).

The most successful people in business and industry are the best pickers of men. They employ the best brains and utilize the benefits of mastermind alliances for their own advantage. Thomas Edison was hard of hearing (partly deaf) and was labeled untrainable by his teachers but he surrounded himself with the best brains in science and engineering. History has recorded him as the man who invented the electric bulb, even though he could not have achieved that without using other people's brains.

Other times, in fulfillment of the mastermind principle, you also need to use other people's money. By doing so, you leverage the wisdom of those contributing to your success in life and enterprise.

Scripture is replete with stories of men who became elevated by critical mastermind alliances. Proverbs 13:20 sums it up: "He that walketh with wise men shall be wise: but a companion of fools shall be destroyed."

- Lot came to wealth and abundance based on his association with Abraham.

- Joshua was elevated to leadership status as he served faithfully under his master Moses.

- Elisha diligently accompanied Elijah in ministry and ended up receiving a double portion of Elijah's anointing.

- David's association with a band of vagabonds elevated them from being nonentities to being mighty men of valour.

- Jesus companied with the disciples. He transformed mostly laymen and people of lowly professions into mighty apostles of the New Testament gospel.

The summary is that who you company with determines what accompanies you.

PRINCIPLE 3:

THE PRINCIPLE OF APPLIED FAITH

"Faith is taking the first step even when you don't see the whole staircase."

The Rev. Dr. Martin Luther King, Jr.

Applied faith is the power of belief. Faith is the state of mind in which one clears himself of all fear and doubt. Faith recognizes no such limitations except those imposed on oneself based on prevailing circumstances or the limitations we allow others to impose on us based on their perceptions of our seeming inadequacies.

It's that either you are walking by faith or you are walking by fear. These elements guide our every action— either positively, by faith, or we shrink and withdraw out of fear. Every person has the ability to control his or her mind. Your mind is the one thing that God has given you absolute control of. Successful people clear their minds of things they do not want and dwell upon the things they wish to achieve because the mind attracts the things it dwells upon. In his brilliant book, *The 12 Characters of Great Entrepreneurs*, author Lawrence Ezisi cites the remarkable testimony of his friend whose travails in the oil and gas business sent him into bankruptcy in 2009. After being scammed by fake oil dealers, his once-thriving business began to head downhill. Here's the rest of the story, which attests to the power of faith:

"… bank funds and monies from an investor were at stake. The investor came after him and then the bank which had been a beneficiary in previous transactions now needed to take their own pound of flesh. They all chased him all over the city; in church, at home, on the streets and even in his dreams."

As he gradually sold his vehicles and assets to pay creditors, one of those he most cherished, his girlfriend, also left him. She went overseas to be married to a secret lover. Time went by and one day he decided to solve his problem the old-fashioned way. He went into prayer, calling unto God each day, sobbing and quoting from the Holy Bible. He went to church. He gave his only car to his church.

And then he began to do what most people in such situations would not do. He took cabs to the top automobile companies and priced out Range Rovers, Bentleys, Toyota Camrys, and other big toys. He visited real estate agents, who showed him around great homes, and he asked them, "How much?" When they told him the sums, he'd say "I'll be back . . . expect me soon for payment."

One day, he got a phone call telling him that his dad had passed away. Being the hope of and eldest in the family, but now with no income, losing a dear one was devastating.

He then took his acts to another level by writing a list of all those he had helped in the past, financially and otherwise, and of his numerous gifts to churches, and he presented them in prayer like a lawyer presents evidence before a jury and a judge. He closed his eyes, saying, "Lord, I am a big-time giver. I am rich in abundance. I receive those contracts worth millions. I receive that Toyota Camry car. I receive that beautiful home."

Then, one night, he got a phone call offering him the opportunity to run a multi-million naira contract, which set him back on his feet again. His creditors also, unbelievably, cancelled his debts. It was all achieved through the power of desire, visualization, and faith in what God can do, even at the last hour.

The mysterious power of faith requires definiteness of purpose backed by personal initiative or purposeful action. Therefore, determine what you wish to achieve, develop a plan on how to achieve it, and determine what you have to pay in order to achieve the goal you have set for yourself.

- Ensure a positive mental attitude free of fear, greed, worry, and anxiety.

- Develop your mastermind alliance with other fellow travelers on the journey to success, which will help to stimulate your definiteness of purpose.

- Tap into their enthusiasm as an object of faith.

Recall the enthusiasm of David in his eagerness to fight against Goliath even though Saul the king had tried to talk him out of his enthusiasm. Borne out of faith and definiteness of purpose, David ensured that Goliath the giant warrior, the obstacle before the people of God to their peace, the battle axe of the Philistines, the giant mountain that seemed insurmountable for so long, was not only defeated, but killed and permanently annihilated from the face of the Earth, such that no other Goliath ever troubled Israel again. This is what applied faith can accomplish.

Notes:

- Every adversity carries with it a seed of equivalent benefit.

- Put your faith in the things you can do and not in things you cannot do.

- The mind has no limitations except those you have allowed, whether they be from the negative influences of other people or from the limitations you have allowed fear to set up in your mind.

- Be on good terms with your own conscience and do not kill off your conscience with negative emotions and a negative mental attitude.

- To create a positive mental attitude, you need to first make up your mind as to what you want.

- Remember that every faith-determined action will be tested.

- Every negative state of mind will destroy faith. Hence, you need to control your mind at all times. Give no room to negative emotions.

- Always think that you can do something about your circumstances and go ahead and do it.

- Accept defeat as an indication that greater efforts are needed, but not as a reason to quit.

- A burning desire is the raw material from which faith is created.

- You need also to believe in yourself.

- Write out all the advantages that your definite major purpose will give to you and let them be your motivations for action.

- Build an atmosphere of success around yourself.

The miracles of applied faith:

Napoleon Hill had a son that was born without the ability to hear or speak (what was then known as a deaf-mute). Napoleon Hill refused to accept that his son was a deaf-mute. Hence, he decided to do something about it. For at least 4 hours a day, he prayed for his son. For the first 18 months, Napoleon Hill's son was not able to hear anything. However, after 18 months of prayers, his son began to respond to sound. By the age of 4, he had developed 65% of his hearing. The balance of 35% was accounted for with the use of a specialized hearing aid that was developed for him.

Doctors had told Napoleon Hill to accept the situation at his son's birth, saying there was nothing any medical professional could do about it. Napoleon Hill responded by saying that the professionals may not have anything to do about it but that he, as the father of the child, had something he could do about it. He took responsibility for the situation, to enforce a change. This teaches that if you don't do something, in connection with your faith, about a thing that poses a risk, it is not applied faith. You may call it wishful thinking.

You must have faith in yourself. No salesman ever sells anything to anybody without first selling it to his own self. You have to believe in yourself and develop the great capacity to believe that you can achieve anything that you set yourself to achieve. Otherwise, other people will talk you out of your definite major purpose, or fear may cause you to shrink and quit before you ever take the first step.

Christians are privileged because they can anchor their faith in the saving grace of God through Jesus Christ the Lord. Hence, the apostle Paul said in, "I can do all things through Christ which strengtheneth me" (Philippians 4:13). Similarly, based on his understanding of the efficacy of the power of God in the demonstration of applied faith, the apostle Paul wrote, "For I am not ashamed of the gospel of Christ: for it is the power of God unto salvation to every one that believeth; to the Jew first, and also to the Greek" (Romans 1:16).

Christians, therefore, have faith anchors and faith boosters in the Word of God. (Romans 10:17: "So then faith cometh by hearing, and hearing by the word of God.") The finished work of salvation and the blood of Jesus which was shed has efficacy not only for the redemption of sins but also for the quickening of the believer. The 11th chapter of Hebrews has a chronicle of heroes of faith which could serve as a quick reference to the power of applied faith.

Every adversity carries with it a seed of equivalent benefit.

- Faith is required to understand that every adversity carries with it a seed of equivalent benefit.

- The suffering of Christ on the cross ended up bringing salvation to billions of people all over the world.

- The story of Abraham Lincoln was full of adversity. However, the result of his adversities was the greatest president America has ever had. No human experience should be considered a complete loss.

- Thomas Edison was deaf and, as a result, he was considered non-trainable. He couldn't attend formal school. However, in the midst of his deafness, he developed his sixth sense, by which he made great inventions. Human problems cause men to develop their minds and therefore they end up attaining success.

"There hath no temptation taken you but such as is common to man: but God is faithful, who will not suffer you to be tempted above

that ye are able; but will with the temptation also make a way to escape, that ye may be able to bear it. " (1 Corinthians 10:13)

PRINCIPLE 4:

THE PRINCIPLE OF A PLEASANT PERSONALITY AND FRIENDLY COOPERATION

"Your smile is your logo, your personality is your business card, how you leave others feeling after having an experience with you becomes your trademark."

Anonymous

A positive mental attitude conditions your emotions; it moderates your facial expressions. A pleasant personality has the attribute of flexibility. A positive person who lacks the quality of flexibility will not be an effective leader, especially when success depends on the cooperation of others. Life is a continuous experience in which one must sell himself to those he comes in contact with. Marshall Goldsmith admonishes: "Be your own press secretary." A pleasant personality has patience with others.

Promptness of decision is linked with definiteness of purpose. In our fast-moving lives, those with sluggish personalities will get in the way of those who are definite with their purpose and moving towards the achievement of their goals.

A pleasant personality learns to hide his feelings by hiding the emotions on his face. A smile on the face, facial expression, and tone of voice are the big three attributes of a winning personality. A pleasant personality develops tolerance and a sense of humor. The person who cannot relax with a sense of humor will end up with health conditions and will alienate himself from people.

Pleasant personalities are good speakers. They choose their words in order not to hurt others. They are versatile and speak with a fair knowledge of the subject they intend to speak about. A pleasant personality has a likeness for others. It exhibits hope and trust.

Physical attributes of a pleasant personality include a warm handshake with a smile and good eye contact.

A pleasing personality avoids the inordinate temptation to win at all costs, which is the root of all human behavioral flaws. We engage in arguments because we want to win a debate. We trash other people's opinions because we want to portray our own opinions as superior. We put down others because we believe that, in doing so, we gain ascendancy. We demonstrate emotions and compulsive behaviors because we want to win.

So, whether we show anger, resentment, or self-pity, it is all rooted in our human urge to win, either by demonstrating with a show of anger how badly the other person has behaved or by demonstrating with a show of self-pity how badly we have been cheated.

When we micro-manage information, we demonstrate our quest to win by withholding important pieces of knowledge from those whom that knowledge may benefit. The thinking is that, in their disadvantage, we gain an advantage, all because we want to win.

These are common, natural tendencies. A pleasing personality rises above the norm and utilizes certain critical steps to ensure that his or her behavior is modulated above the quest to win at all costs. Remember that, in life, "You are rewarded for your behavior and not for your feeling" (Rabbi Daniel Lapin). Therefore, hide your feelings. It is a way of exhibiting good behavior in your interactions with others.

The following steps are helpful in developing a pleasing personality:

- Be thankful

- Apologize when you hurt people

- Quit making excuses

- Develop a listening attitude—learn to hear others and not just yourself

- Try to understand the other person's perspective, in a show of friendly cooperation

- Accommodate other viewpoints but do not consent to biased opinions of others. Say "thank you" to any person who offers advice, even when you are certain that you will not implement the advice given. You can never hurt anyone with a genuine "thank you"!

- When you have done wrong, show people that you are willing to change and that you mean to do it.

- Advertise the new you—be your own press secretary!

- Learn to follow up on relationships—every friendly cooperation needs time to be nurtured into maturity

The apostle Paul admonishes in Colossians 1:10: "That ye might walk worthy of the Lord unto all pleasing, being fruitful in every good work, and increasing in the knowledge of God." And he encourages in Colossians 4:5-6: "Walk in wisdom toward them that are without, redeeming the time. Let your speech be always with grace, seasoned with salt, that ye may know how ye ought to answer every man."

A pleasant personality will not only endear you to people but it will also ensure that on your road to success you will receive all the help you can garner in your everyday journey towards Happy Valley. It was friendly cooperation, based on a pleasing personality, that enabled Jonathan to help David against his own father:

"But Jonathan Saul's son delighted much in David: and Jonathan told David, saying, Saul my father seeketh to kill thee: now therefore, I pray thee, take heed to thyself until the morning, and abide in a secret place, and hide thyself:

And I will go out and stand beside my father in the field where thou art, and I will commune with my father of thee; and what I see, that I will tell thee.

And Jonathan spake good of David unto Saul his father, and said unto him, Let not the king sin against his servant, against David; because he hath not sinned against thee, and because his works have been to thee-ward very good:

For he did put his life in his hand, and slew the Philistine, and the LORD wrought a great salvation for all Israel: thou sawest it, and didst rejoice: wherefore then wilt thou sin against innocent blood, to slay David without a cause?

And Saul hearkened unto the voice of Jonathan: and Saul sware, As the LORD liveth, he shall not be slain." (1 Samuel 19:2-6)

Friendly Cooperation (Teamwork)

The road to Happy Valley has many people travelling on it and you need the cooperation of others travelling on this path on a constant basis.

You cannot be an island to yourself, no matter how knowledgeable you may be. You need the friendly cooperation of others. Imbibe the spirit of unselfish, friendly cooperation as an attribute of a pleasing personality. Cooperation, even in the small ways, can lead to massive end results. Marshall Goldsmith opines: "When you involve other people in your continuing progress, you are virtually guaranteeing your continuing success."

PRINCIPLE 5:

GOING THE EXTRA MILE

"I hated every minute of training, but I said, 'Don't quit. Suffer now and live the rest of your life as a champion.'"

Muhammad Ali

Going the extra mile is the willingness to give more of your effort than what is nominally required of you. It is the principle that makes the time clock irrelevant to a worker because he sticks with the job until the work is done, irrespective of what the official closing time stipulates. Nature compensates those who go the extra mile because nature recognizes it as the law of increasing returns. Going the extra mile provides the opportunity for self-promotion. When one goes the extra mile, you become indispensable and it tends to attract a better compensation for your efforts.

In 1989, when New York City's then-top real estate developer (and the current president of the United States) Donald J. Trump was in personal debt of $900 million and his company, The Trump Organization, owed $9 billion, he heard about the banker's convention that was to be held at the Waldorf Astoria. Trump didn't feel like going and, besides, it was raining on that evening. He was well-known for being chauffeured in his limousine but it wouldn't be a good idea to use his limousine that night, since he needed to appear before the very people to whom he was indebted. Thus, he decided to walk in the rain, covered by an umbrella.

He went in to face his creditors. While most entrepreneurs wouldn't have thought of finding a solution within such a gathering of angry bankers who were trying to get over a recession, that was where Mr. Trump found his solution. Right there, he met the very banker who was sending other real estate developers into bankruptcy.

But that wasn't the main issue. If Mr. Trump had not attended that bankers' convention, maybe you wouldn't have ever heard of the very brand name *TRUMP*. That banker had Trump as the next entrepreneur on his attack list. By going the extra mile, Trump did what had to be done in order to survive and remain relevant to the world. Trump solved that problem because he was able to meet that banker at the right time and dialogue with him. The man is now much richer than he was in 1989 when he was in such debt.

In summary, resist any temptation to try to clear up minor things before you attempt to carry out the heavy tasks. Do not fall for that because, if you keep repeating that pattern, it eventually becomes a habit of always beginning to work on low-value tasks. If you want to fire up your ability to carry out high-value tasks, always focus your thoughts on beginning and finishing tasks that are most important to you first. Concentrate on the 20% of your activities that deliver 80% of your results and in no time you will attain personal success.

Notes:

- Going the extra mile makes you develop effectiveness and efficiency.

- By going the extra mile, you become an expert.

- Going the extra mile enables you to have job protection and job security.

- One can determine one's own wage by going the extra mile.

- Going the extra mile makes you develop a positive mental attitude and a pleasing personality.

- It helps you to develop your personal initiative—you discover ways of doing things better.

- It helps you to develop self-reliance.

- It builds the confidence of others in your abilities.

- It is the only ground upon which you should ask for extra pay.

- It destroys the power of procrastination.

- It makes easy the mastery of the mastermind alliance. As you show genuine concern about the well-being of those in your alliances, they become eternally indebted to you.

- Never let an opportunity go by in which you could be at the service of other people. Nature will reward you for whatever you do for God's other children.

Going the extra mile is rooted in self-denial. It promotes the well-being of the enterprise via the well-being of those who work for the organization and it promotes the aggrandizement of people with whom they share relationships. For the one going the extra mile, his/her gratification is in seeing the blessings of everyone with whom they come in contact in the journey of life.

Christo Wiese, the adventurous founder of Shoprite, is renowned for going the extra mile. In the 1990s,

Wiese's passion for expanding his retail-goods-dealership frontiers led him to explore his flair in Zambia. Wiese, who wanted to open a clothing store in that country, discovered that clothing was sold on the street, by hawkers, rather than in shops. Wiese recalled during an interview with South Africa's *Leadership* magazine that, to dissuade Wiese from carrying on with his plans, a colleague told him, "You know, we can't come and open shops here because people prefer to buy their clothes from hawkers."

An undeterred Wiese couldn't be stopped. He simply went ahead and launched a Pep Store in Zambia. That very store turned into a success story like every other store he has opened on the continent.

Fundamental scriptural examples

Abraham had gone the extra mile when he had offered Lot first choice of the land where he would settle, but their herdsmen had a misunderstanding that almost tore the family apart.

"And the land was not able to bear them, that they might dwell together: for their substance was great, so that they could not dwell together.

And there was a strife between the herdmen of Abram's cattle and the herdmen of Lot's cattle: and the Canaanite and the Perizzite dwelled then in the land.

And Abram said unto Lot, Let there be no strife, I pray thee, between me and thee, and between my herdmen and thy herdmen; for we be brethren.

Is not the whole land before thee? separate thyself, I pray thee, from me: if thou wilt take the left hand, then I will go to the right; or if thou depart to the right hand, then I will go to the left.

And Lot lifted up his eyes, and beheld all the plain of Jordan, that it was well watered everywhere, before the LORD destroyed Sodom and Gomorrah, even as the garden of the LORD, like the land of Egypt, as thou comest unto Zoar.

Then Lot chose him all the plain of Jordan; and Lot journeyed east: and they separated themselves the one from the other." (Genesis 13:6-11)

One would have expected Abraham to choose his location first, as he was the elder and a mentor to Lot. He could easily have made the demarcation and ordered Lot to move but he went the extra mile by asking Lot to make his choice first and offering as much liberty as he did in making that choice.

Many times, we renege our rights in a quest to win the love and affection of people with whom we share a relationship. That is simply going the extra mile. When we deliberately play the fool in order to get things going in a peaceful manner, it is going the extra mile. When you service the need of an undeserving client or customer despite his/her irritating behavior, it is going the extra mile. When you do your job not just to earn a paycheck but to ensure that someone is blessed by your work, it is going the extra mile and God surely knows how to reward those who go the extra mile.

Joseph, in prison and unjustly punished for an offense he never committed, obviously went the extra mile when he went over to check what was making some fellow prisoners very sad and depressed. Why should he care, you may ask. He had enough trouble of his own, having been sold into slavery by his brothers and now, to make matters worse, suffering incarceration in prison for a crime he never committed.

He ideally should have had enough food for thought about his own circumstances but he did not allow that to cloud his affection for the well-being of others. He went the extra mile and, with that singular act, God used it as an opportunity to get Joseph recommended to Pharaoh two years down the line. His good deed was remembered.

"And it came to pass after these things, that the butler of the king of Egypt and his baker had offended their lord the king of Egypt.

And Pharaoh was wroth against two of his officers, against the chief of the butlers, and against the chief of the bakers.

And he put them in ward in the house of the captain of the guard, into the prison, the place where Joseph was bound.

And the captain of the guard charged Joseph with them, and he served them: and they continued a season in ward.

And they dreamed a dream both of them, each man his dream in one night, each man according to the interpretation of his dream, the butler and the baker of the king of Egypt, which were bound in the prison.

And Joseph came in unto them in the morning, and looked upon them, and, behold, they were sad.

And he asked Pharaoh's officers that were with him in the ward of his lord's house, saying, Wherefore look ye so sadly to day?

And they said unto him, We have dreamed a dream, and there is no interpreter of it. And Joseph said unto them, Do not interpretations belong to God? tell me them, I pray you.

And the chief butler told his dream to Joseph, and said to him, In my dream, behold, a vine was before me;

And in the vine were three branches: and it was as though it budded, and her blossoms shot forth; and the clusters thereof brought forth ripe grapes:

And Pharaoh's cup was in my hand: and I took the grapes, and pressed them into Pharaoh's cup, and I gave the cup into Pharaoh's hand.

And Joseph said unto him, This is the interpretation of it: The three branches are three days:

Yet within three days shall Pharaoh lift up thine head, and restore thee unto thy place: and thou shalt deliver Pharaoh's cup into his hand, after the former manner when thou wast his butler.

But think on me when it shall be well with thee, and shew kindness, I pray thee, unto me, and make mention of me unto Pharaoh, and bring me out of this house." (Genesis 40:1-14)

The reward:

"Then spake the chief butler unto Pharaoh, saying, I do remember my faults this day:

Pharaoh was wroth with his servants, and put me in ward in the captain of the guard's house, both me and the chief baker:

And we dreamed a dream in one night, I and he; we dreamed each man according to the interpretation of his dream.

And there was there with us a young man, an Hebrew, servant to the captain of the guard; and we told him, and he interpreted to us our dreams; to each man according to his dream he did interpret.

And it came to pass, as he interpreted to us, so it was; me he restored unto mine office, and him he hanged.

Then Pharaoh sent and called Joseph, and they brought him hastily out of the dungeon: and he shaved himself, and changed his raiment, and came in unto Pharaoh." (Genesis 41:9-14)

"And the thing was good in the eyes of Pharaoh, and in the eyes of all his servants.

And Pharaoh said unto his servants, Can we find such a one as this is, a man in whom the Spirit of God is?

And Pharaoh said unto Joseph, Forasmuch as God hath shewed thee all this, there is none so discreet and wise as thou art:

Thou shalt be over my house, and according unto thy word shall all my people be ruled: only in the throne will I be greater than thou." (Genesis 41:37-40)

I dare to say that going the extra mile to sow seeds of goodness will never reduce you because it is governed by a supernatural law that says, "Be not deceived; God is not mocked: for whatsoever a man soweth, that shall he also reap" (Galatians 6:7).

PRINCIPLE 6:

PERSONAL INITIATIVE

"Success depends in a very large measure upon individual initiative and exertion, and cannot be achieved except by a dint of hard work."

Anna Pavlova, 19th-century Russian prima ballerina

The desire to apply personal initiative is the root of all inventions made by man. It is the attribute of breaking away from the norm, not in a quest to introduce chaos, but in a bid to break through the status quo by way of disruptive thinking that creates a new normal. Definiteness of purpose and the principle of applied faith help an individual to develop personal initiative. When you go the extra mile, you also develop personal initiative.

The habit of personal initiative starts its application in the small and unimportant things in life. Personal initiative finds expression when you ask the question: Why not? When circumstances set boundaries for and create limitations on our paths, personal initiative says that there must be a way out. Indeed, personal initiative compels one to constantly seek ways of making improvements to existing norms. It is the mother of creative vision and, more often than not, it requires the individual to go the extra mile in the attainment of his/her set objective.

By way of personal initiative, people have made good out of their seemingly unpleasant circumstances.

Through his personal initiatives, Reginald Mengi, a Tanzanian who used to bed down with cattle, chickens, and his parents in a small mud hut, is now one of Africa's successful entrepreneurs. Coming from an impoverished background, he swore to give back to his family in a big way. So, he set out to work.

Mengi's initial bright entrepreneurial journey began the very day he went to buy a pen but couldn't find one. He simply decided to become a pen manufacturer. From his days of meager beginnings, that small business has now transitioned into a multinational company in diverse sectors.

Even though the proud and the arrogant may question your expression of personal initiative, if it brings about process improvement and the well-being of others, just like Mengi you will soon be celebrated.

Key points in the expression of personal initiative:

- It should be focused on solving a clearly identified problem

- There should be minimal or no collateral damage

- It should provide some improvement to an existing norm

- The impact should be both socially and morally acceptable

- It does not have to make sense to the casual observer

- Allow the result to speak for itself

Abigail used her personal initiative, in 1 Samuel, chapter 25, to remedy what was to be a very bad situation for her family:

"And there was a man in Maon, whose possessions were in Carmel; and the man was very great, and he had three thousand sheep, and a thousand goats: and he was shearing his sheep in Carmel.

Now the name of the man was Nabal; and the name of his wife Abigail: and she was a woman of good understanding, and of a beautiful countenance: but the man was churlish and evil in his doings; and he was of the house of Caleb.

And David heard in the wilderness that Nabal did shear his sheep.

And David sent out ten young men, and David said unto the young men, Get you up to Carmel, and go to Nabal, and greet him in my name:

And thus shall ye say to him that liveth in prosperity, Peace be both to thee, and peace be to thine house, and peace be unto all that thou hast.

And now I have heard that thou hast shearers: now thy shepherds which were with us, we hurt them not, neither was there ought missing unto them, all the while they were in Carmel.

Ask thy young men, and they will shew thee. Wherefore let the young men find favour in thine eyes: for we come in a good day: give, I pray thee, whatsoever cometh to thine hand unto thy servants, and to thy son David.

And when David's young men came, they spake to Nabal according to all those words in the name of David, and ceased.

And Nabal answered David's servants, and said, Who is David? and who is the son of Jesse? there be many servants now a days that break away every man from his master.

Shall I then take my bread, and my water, and my flesh that I have killed for my shearers, and give it unto men, whom I know not whence they be?

So David's young men turned their way, and went again, and came and told him all those sayings.

And David said unto his men, Gird ye on every man his sword. And they girded on every man his sword; and David also girded on his sword: and there went up after David about four hundred men; and two hundred abode by the stuff.

But one of the young men told Abigail, Nabal's wife, saying, Behold, David sent messengers out of the wilderness to salute our master; and he railed on them.

But the men were very good unto us, and we were not hurt, neither missed we any thing, as long as we were conversant with them, when we were in the fields:

They were a wall unto us both by night and day, all the while we were with them keeping the sheep.

Now therefore know and consider what thou wilt do; for evil is determined against our master, and against all his household: for he is such a son of Belial, that a man cannot speak to him.

Then Abigail made haste, and took two hundred loaves, and two bottles of wine, and five sheep ready dressed, and five measures of parched corn, and an hundred clusters of raisins, and two hundred cakes of figs, and laid them on asses.

And she said unto her servants, Go on before me; behold, I come after you. But she told not her husband Nabal.

And it was so, as she rode on the ass, that she came down by the covert of the hill, and, behold, David and his men came down against her; and she met them.

Now David had said, Surely in vain have I kept all that this fellow hath in the wilderness, so that nothing was missed of all that pertained unto him: and he hath requited me evil for good.

So and more also do God unto the enemies of David, if I leave of all that pertain to him by the morning light any that pisseth against the wall.

And when Abigail saw David, she hasted, and lighted off the ass, and fell before David on her face, and bowed herself to the ground,

And fell at his feet, and said, Upon me, my lord, upon me let this iniquity be: and let thine handmaid, I pray thee, speak in thine audience, and hear the words of thine handmaid.

Let not my lord, I pray thee, regard this man of Belial, even Nabal: for as his name is, so is he; Nabal is his name, and folly is with him: but I thine handmaid saw not the young men of my lord, whom thou didst send.

Now therefore, my lord, as the LORD liveth, and as thy soul liveth, seeing the LORD hath withholden thee from coming to shed blood, and from avenging thyself with thine own hand, now let thine enemies, and they that seek evil to my lord, be as Nabal.

And now this blessing which thine handmaid hath brought unto my lord, let it even be given unto the young men that follow my lord.

I pray thee, forgive the trespass of thine handmaid: for the LORD will certainly make my lord a sure house; because my lord fighteth the battles of the LORD, and evil hath not been found in thee all thy days.

Yet a man is risen to pursue thee, and to seek thy soul: but the soul of my lord shall be bound in the bundle of life with the LORD thy God; and the souls of thine enemies, them shall he sling out, as out of the middle of a sling.

And it shall come to pass, when the LORD shall have done to my lord according to all the good that he hath spoken concerning thee, and shall have appointed thee ruler over Israel;

That this shall be no grief unto thee, nor offence of heart unto my lord, either that thou hast shed blood causeless, or that my lord hath avenged himself: but when the LORD shall have dealt well with my lord, then remember thine handmaid.

And David said to Abigail, Blessed be the LORD God of Israel, which sent thee this day to meet me:

And blessed be thy advice, and blessed be thou, which hast kept me this day from coming to shed blood, and from avenging myself with mine own hand.

For in very deed, as the LORD God of Israel liveth, which hath kept me back from hurting thee, except thou hadst hasted and come to meet me, surely there had not been left unto Nabal by the morning light any that pisseth against the wall.

So David received of her hand that which she had brought him, and said unto her, Go up in peace to thine house; see, I have hearkened to thy voice, and have accepted thy person." (1 Samuel 25:2-35)

The reward:

"And Abigail came to Nabal; and, behold, he held a feast in his house, like the feast of a king; and Nabal's heart was merry within *him, for he was very drunken: wherefore she told him nothing, less or more, until the morning light.*

But it came to pass in the morning, when the wine was gone out of Nabal, and his wife had told him these things, that his heart died within him, and he became as a stone.

And it came to pass about ten days after, that the LORD smote Nabal, that he died.

And when David heard that Nabal was dead, he said, Blessed be the LORD, that hath pleaded the cause of my reproach from the hand of Nabal, and hath kept his servant from evil: for the LORD hath returned the wickedness of Nabal upon his own head. And David sent and communed with Abigail, to take her to him to wife.

And when the servants of David were come to Abigail to Carmel, they spake unto her, saying, David sent us unto thee, to take thee to him to wife.

And she arose, and bowed herself on her face to the earth, and said, Behold, let thine handmaid be a servant to wash the feet of the servants of my lord.

And Abigail hasted, and arose, and rode upon an ass, with five damsels of hers that went after her; and she went after the messengers of David, and became his wife." (1 Samuel 25:36-42)

Ultimately, the personal initiative of Abigail did not only save the lives of the members of her family but it paved the way for her to become one of the queens of Israel and David's wife. Her wisdom and initiative obviously could not be ignored by David.

Similarly, many people in this day and age have made a huge success out of their lives, borne out of their own personal initiatives. To the one who is in obedience to this principle: Nature sees to it that your result is amplified. It is a reward that inevitably leads to your own advancement.

PRINCIPLE 7:

SELF-DISCIPLINE

"Discipline is the bridge between goals and accomplishment."

Jim Rohn

Successful people are guided by values. They have ethics and what you might call a "personal code of conduct." Self-discipline connotes the boundaries we set for our lives as individuals. This principle tells you to think first and then act afterwards. It begins with mastering your thoughts and your deeds. Self-discipline gives you complete control of your emotions.

In his best-selling autobiography *Be My Guest*, Conrad Hilton, the man who cut out a picture of Waldorf Astoria (a hotel that belonged to his former manager, Louis M. Boomer) and gazed at that picture for 15 years until he owned the hotel itself, narrates the habits that equipped him for that acquisition and that set him apart in life:

"It had taken a lot of work, four years of dedicated negotiation, and, even before that, careful planning. It had taken a lot of prayer. During the final crucial days, I had attended church at 6:30 each morning. No matter how late we worked into the night, I started the day on my knees."

To the success-minded person, goal attainment sets the tone for objects contained in the self-discipline toolkit.

The "big four" to control:

- Your appetite

- Your mental attitude

- Your budgeting/time

- Your definiteness of purpose

Quite a number of things will always appeal to your appetite, including the pressure to eat as much food as comes to you, the fleshly desire for sex and pleasure of all sorts, the selfish desire to exact revenge, and so on. But the onus is on you to set boundaries and control your appetite. This is a deliberate effort, as appetite is particularly difficult to tame.

Your dominant mental attitude will also be challenged by situations and circumstances that may want you to tilt towards negativity and thoughts of failure. Hence you must show discipline by promptly recognizing such "red-flag moments." This requires that you consciously place a check on your dominant thought process. Success-consciousness is the only hope a person has to attain personal accomplishments. The Holy Scripture admonishes in Proverbs 4:23: "Keep thy heart with all diligence; for out of it are the issues of life."

Time is an important resource that is not renewable and self-discipline in the management of time is essential for success and personal achievement. Discipline with time helps one avoid the deception of procrastination and also helps one avoid the distractive tendencies of people who have no regard for time. Recognize that it takes the same time for one to succeed and another to fail. The difference is in the level of discipline that each person has applied in the management of his/her time. The scriptural instruction in Colossians 4:5 is: "Walk in wisdom toward them that are without, redeeming the time."

Ephesians 5:16 is more emphatic as it warns: "Redeeming the time, because the days are evil."

In the pursuit of development of robust self-discipline, the wise counsel is to be careful of the object of your desire. The attribute of self-discipline is not developed overnight but rather by steadily working on the definiteness of purpose. Competing options are always presenting themselves to us, seeking our attention or engagement.

Self-discipline is required to keep us focused on our definite major purpose. This is particularly important for people who have tasted some level of success, because they begin to live under the illusion that they can do well in everything they decide to venture into. This illusionary self-belief has led people to make shipwrecks of their prosperity, through bogus and unguided investments that have little or nothing to do with their definite major purposes.

An eye focused on the object of your definite major purpose is a *sine qua non* to the development of self-discipline in the pursuit of career goals and the attainment of success.

How to cultivate self-discipline:

- Keep cool when others get hot. This gives you control over the situation.

- Remember that there are three sides to every argument: your side, the other person's side, and the middle view, which often turns out to be the correct argument.

- Never give a directive to a subordinate when you are angry.

- Treat everyone like a rich relative from whom you expect to receive an inheritance.

- Look for the seed of equivalent benefit in all unpleasant circumstances.

- Learn the art of asking questions for which you must receive some answers, especially on subjects you do not understand. Do not assume that you know or that the other person knows. A good question is "how do you know?"

- Never say or do things, under any circumstance, no matter the provocation, that will hurt another person. If you hurt another person, it will come back to hurt you ten times over. Remember the law of sowing and reaping.

- Develop the habit of friendly analysis rather than unfriendly analysis.

- Watch your tone of voice.

- A good leader is one who completes orders as easily as he gives orders.

- Tolerance is essential in discipline.

- If you can't find something pleasant to talk about, it is better to keep quiet.

- Never engage in any small talk. Self-discipline should be applied in stopping yourself from talking about others, especially in a negative fashion, no matter how compelled you feel to do so.

- Never allow the comments or actions of other people to determine your actions. Let your actions be guided by your definite major purpose.

- Discipline your mind to develop success-consciousness rather than failure-consciousness.

The apostle Paul was one person who wrote and also practiced a lot of self-discipline. See his exhortation in 1 Corinthians 9:24-27:

"Know ye not that they which run in a race run all, but one receiveth the prize? So run, that ye may obtain.

And every man that striveth for the mastery is temperate in all things. Now they do it to obtain a corruptible crown; but we an incorruptible.

I therefore so run, not as uncertainly; so fight I, not as one that beateth the air:

But I keep under my body, and bring it into subjection: lest that by any means, when I have preached to others, I myself should be a castaway."

A major application of self-discipline: Budgeting time and money

You must find out who you are, why you're here, and what you will do to get to your goal. Are you a success or a failure? If you are a failure, you may observe that you have been a time waster.

Failure makes excuses and concocts a number of alibis, but success needs no alibi or explanation. The greatest alibi in failure is the excuse that "I had no opportunity." Take inventory of yourself to identify how you are using your time.

There are two types of people: the drifters and non-drifters. The non-drifters have a definite major purpose and they pursue it. The drifters are always followers and they quit at the slightest obstacle. The non-drifters support their actions with applied faith.

A man's occupation is the basis for his success in life. The non-drifter treats his occupation as a great opportunity for worship. To him, the time clock is not important. The non-drifter controls his thoughts as a mark of self-discipline, but the drifter allows his thoughts to run amok. The drifter is a victim of his negative thoughts and all of the negative influences around him. The non-drifter is disciplined, with a positive mental attitude. Non-drifters spend six-sevenths of their lives on their occupations. Drifters find every opportunity and excuse to take a rest because the drifters are not driven by any definite major purpose.

Definiteness of purpose separates DRIFTERS from NON-DRIFTERS.

- Drifters will quit at the slightest sense of danger, opposition, intimidation or discouragement, while non-drifters will keep on keeping on with a clear focus on their definite major purposes. They develop approaches with which they overcome obstacles.

- Non-drifters are not given to excuses, while drifters manufacture excuses to explain away their quitting.

- Non-drifters recognize opportunities as they present themselves and use those opportunities to achieve their goals. Drifters are blind to opportunities because of the inherent shortsightedness of their views. They do not think deeply. They are easily swayed by emotions and by people around them.

Specifics in time budgeting:

- Eight hours of sleep (important)

- Eight hours of work (important)

- Eight hours of recreation

The first two eight-hour allotments are necessary because nature requires them. Most successes and failures are, therefore, determined by how the eight hours allotted for recreation are used.

Budgeting money is essential for success. Plan your investment and possibly seek avenues for your money to work for you while you are asleep. This also requires the discipline to control your expenditure on objects of pleasure.

The Jewish Talmud recommends that your disposable income be divided into three: a third invested in real estate, a third invested in your merchandise as necessary inventory, and the last third for you to live upon. Self-discipline is required to heed to this wisdom.

PRINCIPLE 8:

CONTROLLED ATTENTION

"Successful people maintain a positive focus in life no matter what is going on around them. They stay focused on their past successes rather than their past failures, and on the next action steps they need to take to get them closer to the fulfillment of their goals rather than all the other distractions that life presents to them."

Jack Canfield

Success is the application of thought power. Concentrate upon the object of your definite major purpose.

Dangote concentrated on the provision of basic human needs. Henry Ford concentrated upon the production of low-cost, dependable automobiles. The Wright brothers concentrated on the development of the airplane. Nelson Mandela concentrated on the fight to end South African apartheid and became an icon of the fight for humanity.

Controlled attention is focused on the definiteness of purpose pursued by applied faith. Effective concentration requires that attention be controlled towards the achievement of one's definite major purpose. It requires self-discipline and control of one's mind directed towards a given goal.

One man with clarity of purpose, who knew exactly what he wanted to achieve, was Sam Walton. Sam Walton, founder of Walmart, the largest chain of retail stores in the world, displayed the act of thinking big. There was a group of eight small, regional discount-store chains whose executives met several times a year to share ideas on how to improve their operations. None of their stores were in competition with each other, as they were in different geographical locations. They usually held their meetings in one of the best stores of that group of eight. The group would visit the store, analyze it, and then share its observations with the company's leadership team.

At the end of one of the meetings in 1971, one of the CEOs thought it would be interesting to hear what each person in the group thought his or her company's sales would be in ten years. The first CEO said that his sales had been $40 million USD in the previous year and he thought they could make up to $80 million in a decade. The next said that his company's sales were $60 million and he expected them to be at $100 million in ten years. Another said that sales were already at $100 million and he believed his stores could reach $160 million in that period.

Finally, it was Sam's turn to speak. Sam opened his mouth and said that Walmart's sales were at $44 million and he expected that in ten years they would reach $2 billion. Everyone laughed hard. They didn't know Sam was serious. The man saw what they couldn't see. Ten years later, Walmart's sales exceeded $2 billion. That is how a $2-billion dream can come to light: by thinking big about the future and having the nerve to speak your mind to anyone who cares to listen.

Controlled attention is organized mind power. When directed towards a given object in prayer, it enables one to get connected with God and, thus, delivers the answers that one desires.

Everyday experience in itself teaches us that, no matter how skilled a sportsman is, he cannot be a superstar footballer, a superstar basketball player, a track-and-field champion, and an Olympic gold medalist in boxing all at the same time. Almost all superstars in sports concentrate on and excel in only in one career area at a time, in obedience to the principle of controlled action.

This should guide everyone who aspires to the attainment of success in life to pursue their definite major purpose with focus and controlled action, tailored daily towards a specific goal until that goal is achieved. If possible, further action should be aimed at expanding the horizon in the same business or career that fulfills the definite major purpose.

The science of controlled attention shows that, whatever the brain focuses on long enough, the subconscious picks up and it is acted upon even when the individual is asleep. This is the genesis of specialization that ensures that someone is an expert in his/her endeavour and that makes that person a success in their chosen vocation or career.

Focused attention teaches that one must make a deliberate effort to fight competing opportunities, especially when such opportunities are outside of a person's definite major purpose.

Bill Gates is one of the richest people in the world and has maintained that status for many years by focusing only on software development and on growing Microsoft's tech business. A good number of his contemporaries have split themselves and their focus into many areas of industry, yet Bill Gates has remained richer than all for many years running.

Jesus, in His earthly ministry, declared in Matthew 15:24: "I am not sent but unto the lost sheep of the house of Israel."

So, even though He demonstrated mighty abilities to save and to deliver, He restricted his three years of earthly ministry to the region of the Jews. With that focused attention, Jesus made his mark among them.

Similarly, the apostle Paul recognized that he was sent to minister to the Gentiles, to witness Christ to them. Throughout his many missionary journeys, his attention was focused on the nations outside of the Jews' territory. Hear his own testimony in Romans 15:16: "That I should be the minister of Jesus Christ to the Gentiles, ministering the gospel of God, that the offering up of the Gentiles might be acceptable, being sanctified by the Holy Ghost."

These men, whose work was focused on fulfilling their definite major purposes, continue to impact our world today, even after having departed this earth more than 2000 years ago.

PRINCIPLE 9:

ENTHUSIASM

"The secret of genius is to carry the spirit of the child into old age, which means never losing your enthusiasm."

Aldous Huxley

"A mediocre idea that generates enthusiasm will go further than a great idea that inspires no one."

Mary Kay Ash

The English word "enthusiasm" originates from Greek and means "possessed by the gods." Enthusiasm is a display of intense inspiration or intense religious fervor or emotion. When you turn on enthusiasm, you send out thoughts that affect other people, because there is a spiritual attribute to your enthusiasm.

Enthusiasm is very contagious and tends to capture the minds of people under its influence.

Charles Darrow, the inventor of Monopoly, became the first millionaire board game designer in history not just because Parker Brothers bought the rights to produce the game on a large scale, but because of Darrow's own enthusiastic and persuasive skills in marketing the game. Parker Brothers, which had initially rejected the game, later had to reconsider its decision when it discovered the large orders that Darrow himself had started taking from department stores.

Enthusiasm is one of the most important traits of leadership. When you get introduced to somebody, you have an opportunity to express enthusiasm.

When you meet a stranger:

- Turn on your enthusiasm.

- When you shake a stranger's hand, make it firm and do it with warmth.

- Follow through with questions that engage the attention of the person.

- The best doctors say that the enthusiasm they carry into examination rooms brings more healing to their patients than the medicine they prescribe.

Prayers offered with enthusiasm bring quicker results. Teachers who teach their subjects with enthusiasm communicate their subjects better and gain the attention of the audience, their students.

A positive mental attitude is required in the expression of enthusiasm. Enthusiasm thrives in positive thoughts and actions.

When faced with an interview panel or with making a presentation to pitch a product or service, the level of enthusiasm with which you make your presentation determines, to a large extent, whether or not you will be hired.

Enthusiasm is expressed in the tone of your voice, the expression on your face, and the demonstration of your personal carriage. It is so vital to win the admiration of people with whom you have to cooperate in the journey to success.

The enthusiasm of David convinced Saul to allow him to battle Goliath, to the extent that Saul removed his armour as a king and put it upon David. He was determined to give the young man a chance, having seen his enthusiasm.

Caution:

- Be careful not to demonstrate too much enthusiasm—it makes people commit beyond their capacities.

- The enthusiastic may be misunderstood as arrogant or proud. Therefore, demonstrate enthusiasm with humility.

- While demonstrating enthusiasm, do not completely overlook the odds so that you can make adequate plans to overcome the obstacles that will meet with you on the road to success.

Enthusiasm is an attribute of faith. It is comprised of the belief in self and the belief in divine assistance towards the accomplishment of one's definite major purpose. Joshua and Caleb, talking about the land of Canaan where they had gone to spy, not only demonstrated faith but also showed enthusiasm when they said, "Let us go up at once and possess it, for we are well able to overcome it" (Numbers 13:30).

Despite the evil report of their ten other companions, they stood in enthusiasm, to still the people and urge them to advance at once. It is therefore not strange that the Greeks think of an enthusiastic person as one who is possessed by the gods. Scripture confirms that Joshua and Caleb had a different spirit (Numbers 14:24).

"And they returned from searching of the land after forty days.
And they went and came to Moses, and to Aaron, and to all
the congregation of the children of Israel, unto the wilderness of

Paran, to Kadesh; and brought back word unto them, and unto all the congregation, and shewed them the fruit of the land.

And they told him, and said, We came unto the land whither thou sentest us, and surely it floweth with milk and honey; and this is the fruit of it.

Nevertheless the people be strong that dwell in the land, and the cities are walled, and very great: and moreover we saw the children of Anak there.

The Amalekites dwell in the land of the south: and the Hittites, and the Jebusites, and the Amorites, dwell in the mountains: and the Canaanites dwell by the sea, and by the coast of Jordan.

And Caleb stilled the people before Moses, and said, Let us go up at once, and possess it; for we are well able to overcome it." (Numbers 13:25-30)

PRINCIPLE 10:

LAW OF CREATIVE VISION

"Dream lofty dreams, and as you dream, so you shall become. Your vision is the promise of what you shall one day be, your ideal is the prophecy of what you shall at last unveil."

James Lane Allen

Successful people stand for something: their vision. They have a mind's eye that has created an object of their definite major purpose. This image, created in their mind, is what is termed "vision" and that is what they pursue to actualize, to bring to the realm of physical reality. So, what begins as a synthetic image ends up being a physical object that all can behold and identify with.

Walt Disney created the magnificent Disney mountains in his mind and called in designers and the engineers to discuss the idea. They were fascinated by the idea, the image, and went to work on it. Walt Disney did not live to see it completed but, today, what had been conceived in his mind is now a reality that annually attracts thousands of visitors from across the world. It is a fascinating mountain range, built with steel and concrete. At its inauguration, the person on the microphone said he wished Walt Disney had lived to see the project completed. Walt Disney's widow corrected him, saying that Disney had actually seen in it in his mind before any of them had seen the mountain range before them that day. That is the power of creative vision. Disney's widow understood it better than those who had built it.

The law of creative vision is rooted in a positive mental attitude. The power of synthetic imagination is what aided Thomas Edison in his invention of the electric lightbulb. Creative vision is birthed from a burning desire and a definite major purpose. "Possibility mentality" brings about creative vision and this helps one to see opportunities in the midst of adversity and failures.

How to empower creative vision:

- Follow your inspiration.

- Stop selling yourself short.

- Keep your imagination as sharp as a knife's edge.

- Keep your body healthy with good nourishment and rest.

- Engage in times of meditation, to nurture the emergence of creative vision and the power of synthetic imagination.

- Free your mind from negative thoughts and negative emotions.

- Communicate your vision to the right audience and seize every opportunity to advance your vision, leveraging mastermind alliances.

- Where possible, create physical replicas of objects of your vision. This is why architects create models to show us what final buildings will look like. The physical replicas become inspirational, relating the obvious benefits of your vision in a more physical way.

Nehemiah was a man who demonstrated creative vision and ensured that his vision was actualized through mastermind alliances, enthusiasm, and controlled attention.

At the inception of his vision, he communicated the same to the king, he built an alliance, and, with a focused attention, he went about the business of rebuilding the broken walls of Jerusalem, not minding the distractions and schemes of Sanballat and Tobiah.

The vision:

"And said unto the king, Let the king live forever: why should not my countenance be sad, when the city, the place of my fathers' sepulchres, lieth waste, and the gates thereof are consumed with fire?

Then the king said unto me, For what dost thou make request? So I prayed to the God of heaven.

And I said unto the king, If it please the king, and if thy servant have found favour in thy sight, that thou wouldest send me unto Judah, unto the city of my fathers' sepulchres, that I may build it." (Nehemiah 2:3-5)

The mastermind alliance:

"Then said I unto them, Ye see the distress that we are in, how Jerusalem lieth waste, and the gates thereof are burned with fire: come, and let us build up the wall of Jerusalem, that we be no more a reproach.

Then I told them of the hand of my God which was good upon me; as also the king's words that he had spoken unto me. And they said, Let us rise up and build. So they strengthened their hands for this good work." (Nehemiah 2:17-18)

The test of vision and the resolve of faith:

"But when Sanballat the Horonite, and Tobiah the servant, the Ammonite, and Geshem the Arabian, heard it, they laughed us to scorn, and despised us, and said, What is this thing that ye do? will ye rebel against the king?

Then answered I them, and said unto them, The God of heaven, he will prosper us; therefore we his servants will arise and build: but ye have no portion, nor right, nor memorial, in Jerusalem." (Nehemiah 2:19-20)

The mockery of faith:

"But it came to pass, that when Sanballat heard that we builded the wall, he was wroth, and took great indignation, and mocked the Jews.

And he spake before his brethren and the army of Samaria, and said, What do these feeble Jews? will they fortify themselves? will they sacrifice? will they make an end in a day? will they revive the stones out of the heaps of the rubbish which are burned?

Now Tobiah the Ammonite was by him, and he said, Even that which they build, if a fox go up, he shall even break down their stone wall." (Nehemiah 4:1-3)

The accomplishment of vision through faith:

"So the wall was finished in the twenty and fifth day of the month Elul, in fifty and two days.

And it came to pass, that when all our enemies heard thereof, and all the heathen that were about us saw these things, they were much cast down in their own eyes: for they perceived that this work was wrought of our God." (Nehemiah 6:15-16)

Causes of failure:

- Inability to get along with other people.

- The habit of quitting when the going is hard. Instead of quitting in the face of an obstacle, one should turn on a greater willpower to succeed.

- Procrastination. The man who cannot make up his mind quickly, despite all available evidence, will also quit very quickly in the face of an obstacle.

PRINCIPLE 11:

ACCURATE THINKING

"Without data, you're just another person with an opinion."

W. Edwards Deming

Accurate thinking is comprised of deductive reasoning and inductive reasoning.

In inductive reasoning, facts are not available, so you base your thinking on hypothesis. Deductive reasoning is based on facts and imperial evidence.

You need to know that, having arrived at the facts, you must separate them into important and non-important facts.

Important facts and non-important facts:

Important facts are the facts that may lead you to achieving your definite major purpose, while non-important facts, even though they are verifiable by evidence, do not in any way add value to your definite major purpose. The advice is that you simply recognize that the non-important facts exist but that you do not pay any serious attention to their existence. You simply do not let non-important facts preoccupy you.

Ndidi Nwuneli, a social entrepreneur and founder of Leap Africa, a leadership, ethics, entrepreneurship coaching service provider, is a good example of an accurate thinker. Based on deductive findings, she discovered that 40-60% of the fruits and vegetables grown and harvested by small-holder farmers in Nigeria are wasted annually and that 90% of the processed food consumed in the country is imported.

That information was enough to put her in business. In 2008 she and her husband, Mezue Nwuneli, co-founded an agro-processing company called AACE Foods.

Ndidi, who is also the founder of Sahel Capital Partners, a leading advisory firm, also empowers women across Africa through her company Leap Africa. In an interview in 2013, she cited a survey, conducted by the Small and Medium Scale Enterprise Development Agency of Nigeria (SMEDAN) and the National Bureau of Public Statistics, which revealed a very low level of business-leverage capacity among women in Nigeria. The survey stated that 42% of the microenterprises in the country are owned by female entrepreneurs, while only 13.5% of the small- and medium-scale enterprises (SMEs) are owned by women, indicating that women struggle with business growth. This was information that helped to arm Nwuneli in her establishment of AACE Foods.

And what does this tell the entrepreneur? It is simple: Always look for evidence to toss out feelings of anxiety, doubt, and ill beliefs before you make a business decision or draw up a conclusion.

The other obstacle to accurate thinking is opinions. Be very careful about opinions because they are often based on biases, emotions, prejudices, and selfish motives. Therefore, do not treat opinions as facts. Do not base your thinking on vague opinions.

Notes:

- Always decide to investigate an opinion before it is treated as fact.

- Always seek proof.

- Be careful about slander and negative opinions because they are often biased.

- Scrutinize every piece of information that you get from the radio or TV before you treat it as fact.

- Always ask the person who is giving their opinion: "How do you know?"

- Learn to be cautious and to use your own judgment.

- Be careful about fanatics, as they are often laden with emotions that lead to biases.

- Always ascertain the motive for every statement.

- Be careful accepting opinions from overzealous people. They are often carried away by their own emotions.

Scriptural application:

Solomon is a perfect example of an accurate thinker and he was recognized as the wisest person that ever lived. On a certain day that he was presented with an emotion-laden situation, he recognized it with his accurate thinking and was able to pass the right judgement. The story is quite compelling:

"Then came there two women, that were harlots, unto the king, and stood before him.

And the one woman said, O my lord, I and this woman dwell in one house; and I was delivered of a child with her in the house.

And it came to pass the third day after that I was delivered, that this woman was delivered also: and we were together; there was no stranger with us in the house, save we two in the house.

And this woman's child died in the night; because she overlaid it.

And she arose at midnight, and took my son from beside me, while thine handmaid slept, and laid it in her bosom, and laid her dead child in my bosom.

And when I rose in the morning to give my child suck, behold, it was dead: but when I had considered it in the morning, behold, it was not my son, which I did bear.

And the other woman said, Nay; but the living is my son, and the dead is thy son. And this said, No; but the dead is thy son, and the living is my son. Thus they spake before the king.

Then said the king, The one saith, This is my son that liveth, and thy son is the dead: and the other saith, Nay; but thy son is the dead, and my son is the living.

And the king said, Bring me a sword. And they brought a sword before the king.

And the king said, Divide the living child in two, and give half to the one, and half to the other.

Then spake the woman whose the living child was unto the king, for her bowels yearned upon her son, and she said, O my lord, give her the living child, and in no wise slay it. But the other said, Let it be neither mine nor thine, but divide it.

Then the king answered and said, Give her the living child, and in no wise slay it: she is the mother thereof.

And all Israel heard of the judgment which the king had judged; and they feared the king: for they saw that the wisdom of God was in him, to do judgment." (1 Kings 3:16-28)

Solomon recognized bias, lies, and prejudice for what they were and was able to rule as one of the most effective kings in Israel.

Jesus also could not be swayed by the opinion of men. In John 2:23-25, the Bible records clearly that, even though men believed in Him based on the miracles they saw Him manifest, He did not commit himself to them, for He could obviously see through their biases and prejudice.

In Mark 14:27-31, Jesus predicted that His disciples and all others would deny Him. Peter argued that he would not and was very fanatical about it. It is common knowledge that, at the end of the day, Peter denied Jesus before He was taken to be crucified. This reiterates the fact we must be careful about people's opinions, no matter how vehemently the opinions are expressed.

"And Jesus saith unto them, All ye shall be offended because of me this night: for it is written, I will smite the shepherd, and the sheep shall be scattered.

But after that I am risen, I will go before you into Galilee.

But Peter said unto him, Although all shall be offended, yet will not I.

And Jesus saith unto him, Verily I say unto thee, That this day, even in this night, before the cock crow twice, thou shalt deny me thrice.

But he spake the more vehemently, If I should die with thee, I will not deny thee in any wise. Likewise also said they all." (Mark 14:27-31)

Therefore, as was stated earlier, the only facts to consider are those that are in sync with your definite major purpose. The apostle Paul summarizes the themes of accurate thinking in Philippians 4:8: "Finally, brethren, whatsoever things are true, whatsoever things are honest, whatsoever things are just, whatsoever things are pure, whatsoever things are lovely, whatsoever things are of good report; if there be any virtue, and if there be any praise, think on these things."

PRINCIPLE 12:

MAINTENANCE OF A SOUND BODY

"The higher your energy level, the more efficient your body. The more efficient your body, the better you feel and the more you will use your talent to produce outstanding results."

Tony Robbins

The maintenance of a sound body is essential to success and personal achievement because a sound body is needed to attain a sound mind. Remember the common saying: "Health is wealth." Recognize the mind-body connection.

Sound physical health starts with a positive mental attitude. Sound health starts with sound health-consciousness, just like prosperity starts with prosperity-consciousness. The Kuwei formula for sound health says, "Every day, I am getting better and better." It is important to repeat this to yourself every day, a thousand times.

Do not think with the basis of disease and ill health, for one attracts to himself the things that he dwells upon. Some have become hypochondriacs because they dwell upon thoughts of disease and ill health. Ensure sound eating and maintain an active life with physical exercise.

Requirements for sound physical health:

- Health consciousness

- Eating right with a controlled appetite

- Resting well, as it brings natural healing to the body

- Physical exercise (avoid a sedentary lifestyle)

- Lifestyle modification (free of alcohol, smoking, and all forms of addiction)

- Maintenance of a proper BMI (fighting obesity), as this helps to ensure optimal performance of the heart and the cardiovascular system of the body

- Ensure regular medical check-ups for early detection of disease

Scriptural wisdom on a healthy lifestyle

In the beginning, God assigned work to man as a way of ensuring an active, physical lifestyle: *"And the LORD God took the man, and put him into the garden of Eden to dress it and to keep it"* (Genesis 2:15).

He also gave a commandment on what man should eat: *"And God said, Behold, I have given you every herb bearing seed, which is upon the face of all the earth, and every tree, in the which is the fruit of a tree yielding seed; to you it shall be for meat.*

And to every beast of the earth, and to every fowl of the air, and to every thing that creepeth upon the earth, wherein there is life, I have given every green herb for meat: and it was so" (Genesis 1:29-30).

God also set an example of how to take a rest after six days of major work endeavours. He commanded man to rest when He gave the laws to Moses. All these were meant to ensure good health and came with a promise of longevity.

"And on the seventh day God ended his work which he had made; and he rested on the seventh day from all his work which he had made." (Genesis 2:2)

"It is a sign between me and the children of Israel for ever: for in six days the LORD made heaven and earth, and on the seventh day he rested, and was refreshed." (Exodus 31:17)

The Creator has left us instructions to comply with and an example to follow in order to achieve constant replenishment and refreshment of the human body. Wisdom would demand that we pay attention, to promote healthy living. All human successes and achievements are viewed as nothing in the face of a life-threatening health disorder or disease.

PRINCIPLE 13:

THE PRINCIPLE OF COSMIC HABIT FORCE

"Success seems to be connected with action. Successful people keep moving. They make mistakes, but they don't quit."

Conrad Hilton, founder of Hilton Hotels

The research by Napoleon Hills surmised that success comes from a set of established thoughts and actions which are performed consistently until they become habits. Through established thoughts, patterns, and actions, habits are developed.

Positive thoughts attract positive compensation while negative thoughts bring about negative compensation. "For as he thinketh in his heart, so is he" (Proverbs 23:7).

Every thought pattern or action can become a permanent habit. God gave man one major freedom and that is the freedom of choice. You can choose to become whatever you wish to be, through your thought pattern. Your predominating thoughts become habits that control your life. Your predominating thoughts control your destiny.

The law of cosmic habit force develops through the things that dominate the subconscious mind. Every self-made habit can become permanent through the subconscious mind and can become fixations that operate automatically.

A good example of the power of cosmic habit force at work is seen in the amazing story of a man called Tom Monaghan, who founded the famous American chain known as Domino's Pizza. Tom's childhood was rough; he was raised in orphanages and foster homes following the death of his dad when he was only four. Because he was often at loggerheads with his mom, she sent him to a foster home. Monaghan, who struggled through school as a kid, managed to graduate last in his high school class and was expelled from a Catholic seminary. He attempted college six times but never got past his freshman year.

Years later, in 1960, Tom and his brother Jim borrowed $900 and purchased a floundering pizzeria.

Right in the middle of their startup year, Jim backed out, leaving Tom to manage the business all by himself. Tom persevered. He survived two near-bankruptcies and the outbreak of a fire. In 1979, just when he had begun to open new stores, he was sued by the Amstar Corporation for infringing on the trademarked name Domino Sugar.

Amstar won the first round in court, but Tom Monaghan won on appeal. Tom grew up never succeeding at anything and had developed a low self-image during childhood. But discovering his combination of drive and perseverance, his self-confidence grew. He fought his way to success with the consistent mastery of cosmic habit. He won as an entrepreneur. By the time the lawsuit with Amstar was resolved, Tom's consistency had paid off. He had 290 Domino's outlets under his belt. As of 2017, the company had over 5,000 franchised stores in the United States and over 1,000 internationally.

The principle of the cosmic habit force is behind the scriptural exhortation in Proverbs 22:6: "Train up a child in the way he should go: and when he is old, he will not depart from it."

Through training, thoughts and patterns develop which eventually manifest as automaticity mediated by the subconscious. At the point of automaticity, it becomes difficult to change patterns and attitudes. A pattern of success, built over time through a positive mental attitude and definiteness of purpose, leads to strong self-belief, a possibility mentality, and faith, just like the apostle Paul had when he said in Philippians 4:13, "I can do all things through Christ which strengtheneth me."

To someone like apostle Paul, it becomes difficult to think or act in terms of failure, because the law of cosmic habit force is in operation. In general, successful people develop four patterns of automaticity in thoughts. Namely: 1) I am successful (talking about their general mindset); 2) I have been successful (talking about the past); 3) I can be successful (talking about undertaking present challenges); and 4) I shall be successful (talking about overcoming future challenges). It is a thought-habit, developed over time, that motivates and moderates the undertakings of every successful person who is in compliance with the principle of cosmic habit force.

To make the law of cosmic habit force work for you, do the following:

- Write down a plan and set of actions to carry out the plan.

- Set out a definite timeframe in which to carry out the plan.

- Constant repetition of a purpose, under the influence of faith and enthusiasm, will establish a passion that literally will control your every action. A pattern develops in your subconscious mind.

- Always put in your mind that every adversity carries with it a seed of equivalent benefit. This thought pattern builds a habit in you which enables you to scale every adversity, because God made life in such a way that people experience ups and downs.

EPILOGUE

If you have come this far in reading this book, I have a good feeling that you desire to make a remarkable success out of your life and I salute you.

The challenge is that knowing the principles may not be enough. Research has shown that less than 40% of people who receive a lesson actually go on to put that lesson into practice. It is my hope that you will be a part of that small percentage, so that the time you have spent reading through this book will not have been wasted.

A common saying is "success is a choice." What you do with the principles you have learned in this book is critical to the set of outcomes you will get in your life. Jesus Christ, after delivering a major lesson to His disciples, stated in John 13:17: "If ye know these things, happy are ye if ye do them."

Your success and eventual happiness will be incumbent upon what you do with the knowledge you have now received. As you embark on this journey, I have a good feeling that YOU ARE THE NEXT BIG SUCCESS STORY—especially as success is no respecter of age, race, or creed. Success is consciously and willingly attained by those who are passionate in their quests to reach their definite major purposes in life.